Petitions
Petals & Pace

Petitions Petals & Pace

A POETRY COLLECTION

SUMMERS.DEY

I dedicate this creation to
Her, She, & Me...
Heal on...

Contents

Part One

The Many Parts Of...

Summers.Dey

In My Element, Praise God

I make praising him my practice, posed, purpose, and peaceful. I hear his voice in the silence, set apart, which becomes my solitude.

Only to allude to my direction, with divine protection over my life, to continue without strife, doing more than to survive.

Yet, I thrive knowing he on high the very throne of my heart, never to part kingdom created covenant.

I make praising him my practice.

UnSmothered

A gasp of air for it's been so long with all the pile I under there...claim it as life unfair, with the backpack, bean bag, and sachet I carry or wear...UnSmothered

Days deem the night it's been an uphill fight, just for an air bubble...No stranger to trouble as aged on...so many gone, yet Freedom has not become fragrant to my atmosphere... do they dare give an ear...UnSmothered

Foreign is the display, laying down burdens today. Where are my clothespins? Where ends to the meet mends? Why hang out a dry sheet...to decay from continuous sun rays unwarranted...UnSmothered

Fresh wind, breath on me, oxygen provided from the tree along the wall there...without care, I'm breathing.

UnSmothered

Released

Some things are not seeds you need to sow, what may show, or dim your glow...it's time, dear heart, to let it all go...

Feeling swept off your feet, keeping emotions tucked and all neat, sweetie, I want you to know... it's time, time, and time...let it all go...

No longer waste your time or the heart bestow...

When the answers you need will still be a "no"...

Just breathe, baby, and let it all go...

Burdens laid down by night, only to await the sun to shine bright, in that morning light as grace was the tow...I grow...

A blessing in disguise because I let it all go...

Finding My Fire

I was all burnt out; nowhere could I show my zeal was gone, a rancid rain had all but proclaimed the extinguishing; I was all burnt out, with doubt daunting a dance in my head like a two-step cha-cha' while singing ah-ha's who's to blame now...

I was all burnt out, no more hand clapping and clout, no one knowing what you're about. As if they knew, everything that you went through...before...I...was...all...burnt...out... shows as the sun shines in its singleness and sets a flame.

Putting away the shame and any subordinate to light the way. As some might say, rise again, stand stone-faced to the wind that wanders around as you're ignited. Yeah, it's time to get excited; set your face like a flint, girl; you found your fire!

I Can Only Be Me

I can only be myself to remain free...consciously, caring, moment to moment, sharing respectfully...I can only be me; by covenant, I'm covered by the almighty creator not to be saved for later.

Yet deserved and divinely preserved for the now...

No matter how others receive thee...

I can only be me, to remain free flowing in knowing his favor, absent of worldly remnants.

She's Moving

I pray for her; in yesteryears, I won't hold back tears that Free the Phenomenal Feminine Flow...

I pray for her, you know, future to unfold, beautiful stories untold they await thee...

I pray for her; so much to say when you look at her today, she's astounding, heart-pounding, rhythm & rhyme sounding sista' some mistook her for that other woman...

I pray for her, you see, cause that time-traveling queen is me!

I Hear You

I've been listening for echoes lately...not a specific date but words to resonate and marinade from one's memory...whereas that my father said would not lie dead but yet dormant...

I've been listening for Echoes lately, to come back clear in consciousness clairvoyant and calmly all the same; you don't have to admit the words are mine, just as a change from a dime, it doesn't matter...

I've been listening for echoes lately, sound clear as a day's blue sky. I don't have to question why his timing; I'll just keep on rhyming into my future rhythm and listening for echoes.

The Perfect Exchange

I'll give my salt to the sea...as it cleanses me, my heart is heavy and truly needs to be free...I'll give my salt to the sea...for only it will reciprocate with me, the waves that crashed along the way, the breeze beyond on sunshine all day...I'll give my salt to the sea...

Because my peace is the key, let it be...

So clouds and thunder may roll, for many moons my heart they stole, broken pieces remaining...

Daily forecast with-staining a lifelong overcast of reconciled rain...

I'll give my salt to the sea blended beyond battlefields, yet better than any bayou there; it stands in its own birthright of beauty.

The Wrong In Strong

Her strength strips her as she dares to bare all through her nakedness...from caramel to creams, to hugged & kissed by the sun, our battle is yet won, tho our generational genre won't let us overcome the soul shackles, minds baffled, cotton-fields, where songs are sung, couldn't lessen the weight we both carried...she is stripped by her strength, trading beauty for ashes...in this day & time as she removes her false lashes...the words to remain...**that still wasn't good enough**.

World winds demand tough stuff, being buff, not tuff enough, being strong some how went wrong, in the heart of the matter...at the end of the day, soft is simple-but; the pulsating of your left temple plays a much distinctive tune... she is stripped by her strength even when she's given every length of her being as if He's not seeing or trying to uncover & discover her need—that could lead to dismissing her...she is stripped by her strength with the world & worth on her shoulders...she will *shine on* even where situations become shady, with all that is in her...holding face to be accepted as a ***lady***.

Love Potential

awning away, hoping and wishing day by day that you grow to become more than just my bae...love potential when dreams are vivid and widespread, your heart can be lead, longings fed, and the future steadfast...

How long will the ego trip last, building this mask? As many times you ask this love, potential truths come exponentially, maturity, growth, and healthy foundations are essential, and survival is cut short, like riding on a degree with no credentials. While at the same time, all along, you had love for their potential.

Part Two

Passports To Peace

My Son

Shine on...in this life, we have to fight...with wisdom, we remain warriors through the night—so shine on... don't dim your light. Continue to do what's right for your soul's season...God gives us reason each and every sunrise...don't dim your light. Favor or flow may get tight but don't be deceived by entanglement...

Don't dim your light cause Grace and her cousin Joy are around the corner holding choices, chances, and change... yeah, it might feel strange when he starts to re-arrange our fixated furniture...

But he's bright...so, love...don't dim your light...

Cures During Corona

I examined the divine development during this period of chaos, confusion, and what some would define as a sign of the times in the craziness; it occurred past the crap calcified on the conscious, finding themselves cohesively cutting past just on a curve, the cost for a cure for whatever ails you...

It came at a time when countries should've been crushed, no longer having to be rushed down the fire lane of humanity, holding to my sanity, once where I had to cry, crawl, or cut lines while juggling like a jester—leaking and losing all self-respect to the sabotage of systems separating the singleness to survive when comes to healthcare...now they're all in despair...is that your love one over there, hurry somebody better care...now!

No matter what the cost, how many will be lost?

Cures During Corona...

Freedom

What's meant for some, when looking, becomes numb at its essence. Freedom ain't free when you cannot see your way passed Tomorrow, full of shame and sorrow. Would another man understand when you don't have an escape plan in your pocket...

Freedom for me and my mind is the sign of the times just as the wind blows by while dark clouds in the sky aren't so distant...

Freedom after being renewed mentally, released from decade's worth of abuse, putting power to use for the direction of destiny...

Awake—The Spark

Ni**a, you have stayed in the dark way too long, singing that same ole song your forefathers forsake, giving our ancestors a belly ache from the bolls of boats, no way to pass notes, while sending up signs of freedom, resistance to their royalty beat em'...

Let's brand em' we can't stand em' was the anthem in the end. Tell em' we win, for the flow of the river changed, our creator's hand rearranged in the midst of chaos; some called it corona...

No longer the jester nor clown, put that shit down and dust off that crown, my brotha, wash off the blood stains; our time still remains, and there are divine royalties in our veins.

King Up!

Sky High

As a cumulous cloud filled to its fullest capacity, he poured out just like a spout it was directed...divinely protected, as his words projected what was learned and out of his self-concern, he erected his stance...

Not a romantic dance yet an act of love, downloaded from above, brought from brokenness, now to find rest on this promised road, while God himself will unload findings to foundations the pureness in relations according to his will, in time reveal clouds filled with covenant.

The Wind

Wows and wonders go, as moments in a moment tow away sorrow, not one promise for tomorrow...tiny tears like whispers to the ears, where did the years go...slow down as the winds whip around...us...kicking up dust as the past peels back, lack still lingering, as willows to flight on their plight whisk away, only so many hours in a day...

Better make the best of it while the wind within remains.

Run

The great *race* is a social construct...the heart of humanity's origin beats to one drum...

To be human was redefined by people through the distribution of laws, social clauses, & disenfranchisement, all indoctrinated through political agendas generationally oppressing a certain population, which has left them beaten and battered, spiritually splattered, un-nurtured while unfed in blighted areas that appear visually dead in this country. Turn the lights on...

Bring light where things have been tight beneath barren, the deepest and darkest secret places where evil dwells; midnight swells as the moans and the groans of our ancestors yell deep within us; this was their story carried as a torch to ignite the way not to go dim by night, but bring forth the day of true freedom....it is within sight just hold on one more night rather marching, standing or putting pen to pad we must keep in motion...rather mad, sad, or glad this is real resurrected power in this hour of transition.

Mind Your Melanin

As the call to I don't care spewed from his mouth in convoluted colors, the crucification of kinfolk from kings was clear...no matter how much you speak into one's ear, their tone remains deaf...relevant that there isn't much left. Still, surface melanin, a hue of a man, birthed seed from the motherland yet found orphaned... cruelty was the cross to bear, beaten, all the mistreatin', left them star struck, no more self-knowledge to tuck, it had been so long since he tied his camel wrong, what a foreseeable future has gone. Hue man...

This way, you hide...while the last tide to the sea abides unknown...only by his hand...just as cuts of sand, as the moonlight shines in the darkness...yeah, it may look dim, to them, as light within him, is his drum for the heartbeat which restores the rhythm...throne connected keys to your king-dome. Hue man...

Manifestation is your melanin.

Part Three

Poetry Poured Out

Sincere Serenade

Is there anyone out there that is real, real to recognize their royalty and with boldness walk in it, wanting royal, wearing royal, revealing royal, not leaving one's mind to toil, over the trivial things, brothas presenting with rings, not without value...Salutations, developing relations, long-lasting, dimensional castings, covenant.

Is anyone out there real?

M.M.M.

The motivation behind the many media memorials gives way to those whose hair coils naturally, to rendering repetition and another audition of "Emotions being Engineered" while willingly allowing civil unrest to be carefully handcuffed, carried, and carted away as the usual casualty, while the crushing of WE...Soles of shoes, carrying signs spreading news become end credits to thee and those behind the camera they all pose while the lenses of the cause continue to remain out of focus.

#KeepYourConsciousClear
#TheViewImpactsYou

Managing Momentous Moments—While Conquering Your Cross

Resurrected

Overcoming your cross when counting all loss as gain while moving past enormous pain, and the bloodstain banner continues to wave in a whirlwind where it began through...genealogical genocides, as fundamentals of family ride on eternity, disguised in subconscious suicide thought as unbecoming memories...

A series subdued as God's interlude becomes prominent.

Uncovering

Get Naked With Me...
Underneath these layers lie treasures you seek...

Get Naked With Me...
Harbors hide the souls' tides as the waves, you know...untold truths, something our youth designed...

Get Naked With Me.....
Yes, my mind is turning as we're learning in a stopped time...Your destiny met mine...The feel of your body was so divine...

Get Naked With Me....

I Want to Explore Your Wholeness.

Small Breaths

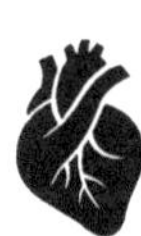

If only for a Moment—you allow my heart to break...
If only for a Moment—you allow us to partake...
If only for a Moment—we love the warmth of your
   precious being, even now unseen...

We thank him...

If only for a Moment—we knew you couldn't stay...
If only for a Moment—we allow God to have his way; on
this day, we wish you your first...

Happy Heavenly Birthday,
My Grandson

Perspective Places

Perspective Places the mess that divides races, leaving traces of generational spaces between loved ones... Perspective Places in the essence of time as we recite never mind...Again and Again, while not to befriend through Kingdom Kinship, a humanistic nostalgic fragrance for the Father...Perspective Places are shown on too many faces on this day. All we can do is pray for father God to make a way, although some will say let me stay...

Perspective Places constantly erase **unity**.

Is This Real

A finally a place to chill, sit still and reminisce a relaxing romance as your soul does a dance in gratitude...Is this real rightfully delightfully mine, sent from the most high, one I didn't have to die to experience...My little piece of heaven...

My Reality Realm...

That Tree

Elders Too Early, unequivocally quiet as a silent riot
arises, shaved yet misbehaved roots go a
wandering...the do's and don'ts of one's diet, with
those that left out the many details...now dormant in
disease...this world bringing many to their knees
everywhere, say a little prayer for the offspring...

Elders Too Early, surely goodness would never say
goodbye, or loved ones tell a lie when the seed falls 'round,
from fertile soil to rocky ground, some weeds grow,
and we never truly know the outcome...

Release & Manifest

Heartache and pain in every negative stain in my soul,
   I release you.
Raw and remnants of relationships that unraveled,
   I release you.
Well-written words that came as wolves in sheep's clothing,
   I release you.
Whoas, like winds and waves that wavered my mind,
   I release you.
Unspoken speeches, feeling & emotions like leeches,
   I release you.
Things that came fast but I could not leave in the past,
   I release you.
Procrastination paces, clutter, and overwhelming spaces,
   I release you.
   I, am **free**.
Abundance, bounty, and beauty,
   I receive you.
Destiny divine already mine,
   I receive you.
Frequency with the flow in my conscious, I already know
true purpose,

Release & Manifest Cont.

I receive you.
Oceans that see as I discover me,
I receive you.
Romance and relationships, pure, positive, and perfected,
I receive you.
New manna manifestations, you are welcomed today Ase'

Priceless Pleasures

Treasure You Don't Trade, the memories and love made in the moments, as if time stood still without movement, it all becomes wonder...Full of favor, every minute to the second we savor, a harmonious high, as we kiss each other good-bye till next time...

Fit For a Crown

(By the Comforter)

I was given this quilt to cover me, but it didn't quite fit, knowing it was knit with squares...

Together it appeared rather rough, with rations of remnants filled with raw edges...

Peace is gathered with love for which never was put above, all the bulls**t, while blatantly blown back by the wind, as I'm so quantitatively covered...

By this quilt, quiet goes, as humility flows, and only God holds the remedy to these well-constructed remnants, cut as sackcloth which clings together, fit to be tied yet torn, leaving love scorned due to the depth of destruction, damp days, the weather full of haze, and no future harnessed for the keeping...

While this quilt kept on creeping past my feet because it didn't quite fit, as I now sit, with no more remnants of squares, shedding of hairs, falsehoods served as cares, no matter how much this heart bares, I'm Covered.

Come Forth...

Transformation and change can always rearrange one's thought process, put inequity to rest, and let the blood pass through, knowing, just not showing from the root, food came a foundation in which the O in your negative separated more than just plasma...Seed for the sower, as the young boy pushed the lawn mower, had dreams of his freedom, footsteps, and future...Can you fathom the fullness forthcoming of your birthright?.. leading those caught in a trap of darkness to king "dome" connected light...Come Forth, Hue-Man; the time has come. All this world's street wars have already been won, divinely deemed multidimensional, melanin manifested, never to be boxed in cause if you knew whom you were created to be, you'd never touch that, speak that, or visit that place again. Come Forth!

In fierce faith, humble heart, presenting reciprocation to whom true Creation designed leaving behind death to resurrection, cause regression begot depression—There Are Many Life Long Lessons—Grand Rising.
Come Forth.

Tears on the Window *Pain*

When clouds are clearing, and your heart keeps steering westward, only the first pings can be heard as the streams of precipitation run salutations so softly, without words, silent chirps from the birds that once flew here, yes my dear, your behavior was all fear, just as the cumulus cloud it's presentation full and loud most times vociferous...

Thunder in the absence of lightning rolling with no destination and droplets as one's outcome...

After a while, you find yourself numb for the shelter sought not to give a waking thought of any aftermath as we take another path...

Tears on the window pane leave reflections of the stain.

Choice & Chains

When I broke free, she was through with me...from long nights, loss of energy, barren zones to moans, and the groans of my stillness, oh I hope you feel this, when I broke free, she was through with me...

Entitled, self-idled on that ego blend, not a heart to mend or thought to, all she knew was what she needed, no matter who else might be deemed depleted in the process, the mess, stress, the disrespect undressed in the wide open, all the while hoping...that third eye would open to a new view because finding you is your Freedom...

About the Author

Petitions, Petals & Pace, the soul-stirring collection of poetry presented by the talented Summers.Dey. Which includes works from her debut publication, The Many Parts Of: Summers.Dey. Petitions, Petals & Pace delves into the multiple stages of life, with thought-provoking chapters like Passports To Peace and Poetry Poured Out. Summers.Dey's captivating writing style will keep you completely engrossed in her work from cover to cover. Hailing originally from Indiana, she now proudly calls Phoenix, Arizona, home.